Rental Property Investing

Create Passive

Income, Wealth and

Financial Freedom

with

Real Estate Investing

Table of Contents

As befitting its nature, it is presented without assurance regarding its prolonged validity or interim quality.

Trademarks that are mentioned are done without written consent and can in no way be considered an endorsement from the trademark holder.

Introduction

Congratulations on purchasing **Rental Property Investing: Create Passive Income, Wealth and Financial Freedom with Real Estate Investing** and thank you for doing so.

Baring the occasional housing market crash, real estate is one of the most reliable types of investing a person can do.

In addition, real estate investment rental properties offer up a reasonable return for very little effort once everything is up and running.

However, getting to that point isn't exactly a straight shot which is why the following chapters will discuss everything you need to know in order to ensure that your first initial venture into rental real estate investment is a successful one.

First, you will learn all about real estate investing and what it is you are thinking about getting into.

Next, you will learn how to find properties that are worth pursuing and also how to find the sort of deals the average investor might miss.

You will then learn how to find the best loan for purchasing a certain property, regardless of what different kinds of banks and loans you currently have to work with.

From there, you will learn about the various considerations you will have as a landlord as well as how to balance your needs against those of your eventual tenants.

Finally, you will also learn all about turnkey rental properties, a true passive income stream as well as various tips for success.

It is important to state that there are plenty of books on this subject on the market so I truly want to thank you for choosing this one!

In addition, every effort was made to ensure that this book is full of as much useful information as possible. Please enjoy!

Chapter 1: Rental Property Basics

When it comes to profitable investment opportunities, there are few choices that are more profitable and reliable when it comes to making money than real estate.

In fact, the idea of real estate investment has been around for as long as there have been permanent structures and the concept of land ownership.

Another testament to the reliability of real estate, when comes to making money, is the fact that it is considered a core part of any properly diversified portfolio.

In addition, real estate is a good investment choice regardless if you are just getting started or if you are looking to add to your preexisting plans for retirement.

One of the reasons that real estate is generally so reliable is that it offers a unique mix of liquidity, cash flow, profitability, net worth and diversification benefits not seen in other types of investments.

Having an understanding of the benefits of real estate investment and understanding how to best put them to use are two very different topics.

However, this chapter will aim to outline the basic principles that are used with real estate investing as well as the various risks involved when investing in real estate.

At its most basic level, real estate investing is all about actively profiting from physical property regardless if that profit comes from using the property in question to make a profit or selling it outright for more than what you paid for it.

It can be said that real estate investing can be ideal for those who enjoy the idea of having something tangible to go along with their retirement investments.

One thing that can be said is that profit from real estate investment typically manifests itself in a few key ways.

The first of these is through the natural process of **appreciation** which some pieces of property go through over time as the market in the area the property is located in changes, and eventually becomes much harder to find.

Appreciation is also known to occur if upgrades are made to the property in question or the area around it receives substantial upgrades to its infrastructure instead.

The second method of generating a profit in real estate investing is via renting out a property that you have purchased in order to see an eventual profit in the long run.

This type of cash flow can be generated from a wide variety of properties including things like office buildings, storage units, car washes, condominiums and more.

A third type of making money via real estate involves profiting from the ancillary services related to your rental properties such as vending machines or washing machines in an apartment complex.

Finally, when you make the decision to become a landlord, you are essentially also making the decision to start a business that is offering rental services to the public and it is important to treat it as such.

As with any new business that means one of your first priorities should be to set up a limited liability corporation to protect yourself should something terrible happen that results in one of your tenants suing you.

Essentially, setting up an LLC protects your personal assets should something bad happen.

Having an LLC will simply help you to go about your real estate investing business without any major worries.

An LLC can be created for a few hundred dollars in under 30 minutes at LegalZoom.com and the benefits will far outweigh the costs in the long run.

Types of rental property to consider

Condominiums: There are several things about condominiums that naturally make them a good fit for those who are just starting to invest in real estate.

For starters, they are likely to attract young, upwardly mobile renters who tend to be relatively low maintenance and also pay their bills on time.

Additionally, you won't have to worry about finding a property management company as one will automatically come with the property.

Finally, all the maintenance and day to day issues are all going to be handled as well, letting you to sit back and collect your profits.

On the down side, however, condominiums generally produce lower overall returns because the rent is lower than it would be on a single-family property while also appreciating at a slower rate for the same reason.

Single family properties: Rental homes are more likely going to attract families or multiple individuals in a stronger relationship than in many other rental scenarios.

This means that the overall amount of income you can rely on the renters having is going to be higher and more overall stable.

Additionally, renters who are looking for houses instead of apartments tend to be looking for something more long term as well.

Tenants in these situations will require and expect more of the property and their landlord, which can sometimes be a little time consuming for a landlord.

At the same time, as a landlord it can take longer to find the right renter and it will also require more work to get the property back to a neutral state after the tenants move out.

Multifamily property: Whether it is a duplex or a small apartment complex, multifamily properties are typically going to generate a more reliable income stream than either a condominium or a single-family property simply because you have a greater group of tenants to depend on.

Additionally, you can typically easily find a property management company, or even an individual to live in one of the units in exchange for acting as your stand-in landlord/property manager on the premises which will serve to negate the need for a rental property management company entirely.

The biggest downside with a multifamily property is that the **quality** of your tenants will be largely based on the types of people the previous landlord rented to.

Real Estate Investing Starter Tips

Tip #1 Property management: If you are interested in generating passive income from your rental properties then you will want to look into hiring a property management company.

Property management companies will deal with tenants directly so you don't have to, which is a big plus for many landlords.

When it comes to using property management companies, it is important to do your research regarding which one makes the most sense for you.

The average cost of a property management company is between 8 and 12 percent of the monthly rental price.

When you are first starting out you will likely need to add as much as an extra 10 percent on top of this cost as very few property management companies are going to be interested in working with a single-family home.

While these fees will eventually drop as you find more properties to rent out, this is likely what you can expect to pay from the start.

Tip #2 Start Small: While many new real estate investors will look to duplexes or even small apartment complexes as ways of starting off investing in rental property, if you are planning on starting with bad looking properties then you are generally going to be better off starting with something smaller such as a single-family residence.

While this choice will often prevent you from using property management companies that prefer larger clients, you will find the benefits of cutting your renovation costs on a more reasonable project to be substantial.

Simply when you are starting off, don't bite off more than you can chew. Instead, focus on learning as much as you can during your first real estate property renovation so you can focus on making as much as you possibly can on your second real estate property.

Tip #3 Know your limits: When it comes to determining what type of real estate investment you can afford, it is important to start the research phase with a clear idea of what your limits are when it comes to cash-on-hand, hard money loans, bank loans or even owner-financing.

Only by having a clear idea of just what you can afford and what it is going to cost you will you be able to accurately determine if a property is right for you or not.

Keep in mind that when it comes to purchasing investment real estate property it is important to always have a clear idea of the amount of money that you can afford when purchasing a property.

In addition, you also want to have a clear idea of the most amount of money that you are willing to pay for a property and you also want to know when to walk away from a property as a result of the property being too expensive.

Even more important is to stick to your guns when it comes to encountering different prices for various real estate properties.

Simply having a plan and sticking with it is what separates the successful real estate investors from the suckers.

Tip #4 Do your homework: Before you take the plunge of investing in real estate it is always a good idea to understand not just the local housing market but also the national housing market and how the two are currently interacting with each other another.

Only by having a clear idea of the state of things from every angle will you be able to accurately determine when a bad property is priced reasonably or if there is still room to negotiate further.

It is equally important to remain aware of exactly the type of financial responsibility you will be taking on when you go ahead and make the purchase of a real estate property.

Being aware of investing in real estate means being prepared, however, and knowing exactly what you should be expecting will make it easier to make a profit in the long-term.

Tip #5 Pricing properly: After you have found a property that seems promising and determined the quality of the surrounding area you can determine if the property is ultimately going to be worth your investment and time.

To do so, start by estimating the amount you can charge for rent based on the research you have done and the amount that similar properties are going for in the area.

From there you have to determine the taxes on the property, payments, the cost of the management company, insurance, and any other payments as well as costs.

Additionally, you will want to include an extra 10 percent of the total rent revenue for the year, in case of an extended vacancy.

With all the costs calculated you simply subtract the difference before factoring in a 3 percent appreciation value.

Once you add up the numbers you should have a very clear idea if the property is worth the investment, or if you are best served by going back and looking at other properties.

Tip #6 Advertising: Once you are ready to rent out a property it is important to do everything you can to ensure the vacancy is filled as quickly as possible.

The day after renovations are completed is the day the property starts costing you money while it is sitting vacant.

When it comes to getting the most effective advertising for a new rental property for the cheapest price, the best place to start is with social media.

You are going to want to start the social media campaign for the property on the day that you start the renovations.

Taking pictures of the property throughout the renovation process will serve as a timeline showing how much value has been added to it through the work you have done.

Having digital proof of these things will help to ease the minds of potential renters as they won't simply have to take your word that specific repairs were done.

Tip #7 Understand your affinity for risk: When it comes to investing in real estate successfully, the first thing you need to understand is that without risk, there is no reward.

For example, a turnkey property is far less of a risk than a property that needs some work before you can rent it out, which is why the price is going to be much higher on a turnkey property than a property that needs to be renovated.

Essentially, if you are a risk taker, you may be more prone to taking risks when making investments in real estate that may not be profitable.

However, when you are a risk taker and your investments in real estate are profitable, then you are going to have a higher general tolerance for risk than someone that is afraid of taking risks and is simply waiting and waiting to make a decision for investing in real estate.

When discussing risk, properties that are going to generate a higher rate of return in exchange for being less of a sure thing are considered volatile and reliable investments are considered non-volatile.

When it comes to investing in real estate successfully, the greater the amount of speculation required at the point of commitment, the greater the amount of volatility that investment is said to have.

While a property that requires a lot of work can definitely generate a larger return, in the end, the fact that you need to accurately predict a far greater number of things from the very beginning means that you will likely want to pick a simpler project for your first real estate investment.

If you prefer a low volatility strategy, then you are going to be able to get by with fewer overall quality real estate investments while a high volatility strategy will involve many more investments overall due to the fact that you have to account for failed risky investments as well.

Chapter 2: Finding the Right Property

Finding the right neighborhoods

When it comes to deciding on where to look for your first rental property, the first thing you will need to consider is if you plan on being an active landlord or having someone else manage the day to day operations of your rental property for you.

If you plan on being the person on call for routine issues with your first rental property, then it is important that you find a property that is relatively close to your own home as driving halfway across town in the middle of the night is never any fun.

On the contrary, if you plan on utilizing a property management company, then you will want to most likely focus on a multi-family property as many management services won't work with just a single residence or a single-family home.

Consider the following tips when deciding on a rental property:

Tip #1 Consider the location: This is more than simply scouting the rental prices of homes in a given area, and it requires a "feet-on-the-ground" or simply doing some foot work approach for the best results.

Assuming you are looking for a rental property with a specific type of tenant in mind, then you will want to head out into various neighborhoods and get a feel for them and the types of people that call them home.

You will also want to take into account the general upkeep and feeling of safety that naturally comes as part of the neighborhood as this will affect how much you can charge for the property as well as the types of tenants you will attract.

When it comes to finding out the real scoop about an area, the best people you can hope to talk to are other individuals who are already renting in a certain area.

Usually, renters tend to be far more open and honest about an area's flaws as they are typically less connected to the neighborhood which makes them less likely to lie to protect the neighborhood's image.

If there are no renters readily available, then you will likely want to visit the neighborhood at several different times throughout the day, just to get a feel for how the local people live and act.

You will also want to ensure that the property tax in the area that you are looking to invest in is less than or equal to the average property tax for other broader areas.

It is important to state that property tax rates can vary dramatically from neighborhood to neighborhood and failing to take these sorts of things into account has the potential to seriously affect your profit margins if you are unlucky.

Additionally, you are going to want to consider properties that require as little upfront work or renovations as possible, because the longer a property stays empty, the longer your money is going to be tied up in the investment and not actively working for you.

When looking for a real estate property it is also important to always go into it with a certain target renter or client in mind.

For a true passive income stream you are going to typically want to stick with renting to families, simply because moving family of four or more people is a lot more difficult than simply one or two individuals moving.

This means that when you are doing research on real estate properties to invest in, you are going to want to consider the amenities in the area, including things such as schools or parks.

Don't forget to check out how the local job market is doing as well, both in terms of its strength right now, but also for major developments that could be coming up in the relatively near future.

Not only can a bad local job market prevent you from buying into an area right before an economic downturn, but if you listen to hearsay rumors, you can get into a new real estate area before positive construction starts that will raise the value of the entire area.

Tip #2 Multiple Listing Service: The first place that you are going to want to look when it comes to finding houses or real estate property that are underpriced is the same place that everyone else is going to start, and that is the **Multiple Listing Service**.

The Multiple Listing Service is a compilation of every single real estate property that is currently being represented by a licensed real estate agent in the United States.

The competition on this Multiple Listing Service site is going to be extremely fierce but that doesn't mean that you won't be able to score a great deal every now and then as long as you are willing to work for it.

First things first, this means that you are going to want to check the new listings very early in the morning (4 a.m. eastern standard time early) and again before you go to bed every night.

In addition, you will always want to pay special attention to properties that are listed on Fridays as they are typically going to have less competition simply due to the fact that people don't like to work on Fridays.

Additionally, you are going to want to be persistent on listings that seem difficult to get a hold of; remember, if you are having trouble, so is everyone else which means most people are going to give up before getting anywhere.

Therefore, it is important to be persistent and persevere and you never know what you might find on the Multiple Listing Service site.

That's right! You never know when a great deal is going to pop up on the Multiple Listing Service site and when a good real estate property does become available it won't last long on the market.

So, this means that as soon as you do come across a good real estate deal that you don't want to pass up on you are going to need to be able to act on it as quickly as possible.

Therefore, contacting the listing agent promptly is very important, as is being able to drop everything and viewing the real estate property as soon as the real estate agent or the owner is available.

Tip #3 Newer market properties: Always look for houses or real estate properties that have just come on the market.

There may be a lot more competition with these types of homes or real estate properties that have just come on the market.

However, you will be able to get a real estate deal that is a better deal than a real estate property that has sat on the market for a long time.

If you are quick and offer the right amount money for the real estate property, you will probably get the real estate property before other investors even have a chance to check it out.

The biggest problem with houses and other real estate properties that have been on the market for a long time is that there is a reason that they have been on the market for a long time.

For example, these real estate properties may have major problems with the guts of the home, or they may have problems cosmetically or aesthetically.

Simply, if these real estate properties are not selling, it may be because they may be in an area that does not have a high cash flow.

If the real estate property has been on the market for months or even years, the chances are that you will have a hard time selling it once you purchase it and try to flip it.

You may even have a hard time renting it out if the area is bad area.

A secondary problem that can come from homes or real estate properties that have sat on the market for long periods of time is vandalism.

Criminals take note of homes and properties that do not have any residents living in them and so they exploit these properties.

Criminals could be using these properties to live in them, vandalize them for no good reason or they could even be using them for illegal activities.

Simply, investing in a real estate property that has been on a market for a long time is one headache that you don't want to deal with.

Motivated sellers

If you are looking to pick up properties for the cheapest price possible, then you may want to forego the Multiple Listing Service site entirely and instead go straight to the source.

Here are some tips for finding motivated sellers:

Tip #1 Finding the right motivated sellers: In order to start the process of finding motivated sellers, the first thing you are going to need to do is to find individuals who are in terrible financial situations.

Luckily for you, this is as easy as going online. Assuming you live in a small city you should easily be able to find local companies that are willing to sell you a list (for only a few hundred dollars) of individuals who are substantially in debt and need to sell their real estate property.

Once you have these details, you will then want to visit your local clerk of the court and cross reference the list of names you have purchased with property records to determine who among them currently owns a real estate property and is looking to sell it immediately.

After you have narrowed your list down of potential individuals looking to sell their real estate properties, the next thing you will need to do is to put together a form of letter to send out to these individuals who are looking to sell their properties.

In this letter, you are going to want to introduce yourself, express condolences for their financial issues and then explain how you are able to help them.

You are also going to want to avoid making an offer outright in the letter but make sure to express interest in meeting face to face and discussing the specifics of the deal you are willing to make regarding purchasing their real estate property.

You also want to make sure to include your contact information and then mail out the letters and wait for these property owners to contact you.

While not every property owner you target will contact you, it only takes a small handful of property owners to follow-up with you regarding selling their real estate property to you.

In general, you can expect about a 3 percent response from interested property owners which means that if you send out 300 letters you can expect about 10 interested parties to contact you.

Tip #2 Courthouse step sale: While not true of every state, oftentimes once the entire foreclosure process of a real estate property has proceeded without anyone to come along and stop it, the property will be auctioned off via a public auction that is referred to as a **courthouse step sale**.

While this auction of real estate property will sometimes literally take place on the courthouse steps, this is not always the case and the specifics related to this information can often be found on the state county's website or in the legal notices section of the newspaper.

The bidding for these foreclosure properties typically starts at the amount that the lienholder in question paid for the property and if no one else bids on it then the lienholder takes it by default.

Depending on the real estate property in question and the amount the original owner owed, this type of foreclosure auction can be a great place to find properties selling for extremely cheap.

However, you are only going to be given limited information on the property in question which means that you might be buying into additional liens without knowing it.

Additionally, you typically won't be presented with an opportunity to see the real estate property in its current state and conditions so it really is quite a gamble.

These uncertainties can be mitigated if you can use the methods outlined above to find information on the properties beforehand, but this is hardly a sure thing and even if you speak with the owners beforehand you have no guarantee that they are going to be truthful when you speak with them or fill you in on all of the relevant details regarding the real estate property.

Nevertheless, sometimes the price for the real estate property will simply be too good to pass up and if this is the case, you will need to have all of the cash on hand to pay for the property if you hope to walk away with the rights to the property properly secured.

Tip #3 Foreclosures: Some real estate investors only purchase foreclosures because they're able to purchase these types of homes and properties at a low cost and then renovate them quickly.

You should figure out whether or not investing in foreclosures would be something that you'd like to take on.

Keep in mind that a foreclosed property is a property that is for sale because the previous owner of the mortgage was unable to make payments on it.

Because the previous owner was unable to make payments, the bank now "owns" it.

The bank does not exactly own the property, but they have taken the property as collateral because they originally lent money to the owner of the property and are now not being paid back by the owner as was agreed when the mortgage was signed.

The major reasons why people end up being unable to pay their loans usually include life hardships such as divorce, health, death or unemployment.

Anyway, this is of no importance to you. You are just looking to purchase the real estate property without having to worry about the unfortunate circumstances that are surrounding why the home is being foreclosed in the first place.

Usually, the process of a foreclosure will begin between three to six months after a borrower has consistently not paid his or her mortgage for one reason or another.

At this point, the lender will issue what is sometimes referred to as a **Notice of Default**, or a NOD for short.

Depending where the home or real estate property is located, the county record's office is notified of this situation, and this record goes public.

In some states, the lender is also required to post an official notice on the door of the real estate property letting the mortgage owner know that he is receiving a **Notice of Default**.

This **Notice of Default** gives the owner some heads up that his or her home or real estate property is in danger of being taken by the lending institution.

The mortgage owner will then enter a period of time known as "pre-foreclosure". Pre-foreclosure typically lasts between thirty to one-hundred and twenty days.

During this time period, the mortgage owner is able to work out a deal with the lending institution so that the homeowner does not lose the home.

You may have heard of a "short-sale" before. A short-sale is when the borrower makes a deal with the lending institution (the bank) during the pre-foreclosure period.

During this time, the borrower is able to put the house up for sale at a price that is cheaper than what is owed on the property.

In this way, the lending institution is "shorted" some money, which is why it is called a short sale.

As someone who is purchasing the property, you may think that there is a profit to be had from purchasing a "short-sale" property because you are only spending money on the difference between what the borrower owes the bank.

The primary advantage to purchasing a foreclosed property is that you'll be able to get it at a price that is cheaper than its market value.

The problem is that the bank is going to be unwilling to sell this property because they want to recover the money that they have lost on this property.

Therefore, it's typically going to take a much longer time to acquire a foreclosed property.

For this reason, some real estate investors prefer to negotiate directly with someone who is going through the process of having their home foreclosed prior to the home being formally be repossessed by the bank.

Some other tips that you should consider when you're looking to purchase a foreclosure property include working with a Realtor who has experience with the foreclosure process, getting pre-approved for a mortgage before you approach any sellers, and comparing homes and real estate properties with one another.

Remember, real estate sellers are going to feel more confident in your ability to take their property off of their hands if you have already been approved for a mortgage.

Lastly, remember that you're not going to be able to negotiate the price of the real estate property with the seller during the closing process when you're purchasing a foreclosure.

Therefore, any problems that exist within the home are going to be exclusively your responsibility, which could drastically drive up the cost of the property if you're not careful.

Tip #4 Inherited homes: About 1 million people inherit a home each year.

Imagine if you are part of the real estate team that gets many of these inherited homes listings?

It may not work out each and every time, but there is definitely potential to help someone sell a home they inherited.

These inherited home sales occur for various reasons. For example, the new owner may not want to move back to their inherited home because the home might be in a poor location or in a bad area. In addition, the person inheriting the home may not want to take the time to fix up the property.

So, what you can simply do is reach out and contact these individuals.

How to Find Inherited Homes

1. Visit the county clerk's website. Look for accessing court records online.

2. Access the public database and housing records for inherited homes.

3. Use an online people search to find the new owners. You will have to pay for accessing

the phone numbers of individuals who have inherited a property.

4. If you don't want to pay for the access to phone numbers of individuals who have inherited a real estate property, you can at least gain the address for the property.

   Once you have the address of the real estate property owner, send a letter to the homeowner inquiring about a potential sale of the real estate property and simply explain that you would like to purchase the property or serve as their listing agent.

Tip# 5 Vacant homes: The US Census Bureau states there are 104 million homes, which were vacant in the first quarter of 2017.

At the end of the second quarter 93.2 million homes were vacant, and at the end of the fourth quarter, 94.5 million homes stood vacant.

Many of these homes are still vacant.

Again, there is a need to find local housing records to obtain the name of the owner of a vacant home or property.

Once, you know who the last owner was, you can begin to track them down or the bank that holds the mortgage.

It may be a few years later, but these vacant homes are not all owned and occupied again. Therefore, it may be worth it to look out for vacant homes and properties as a good real estate investment.

Chapter 3: Paying for a Real Estate Property

Once you have found a real estate property that you feel you can profit from, the next thing you will need to do is to consider exactly how you are going to pay for it.

While paying cash up front for a real estate property is certainly the easiest and most effective option, odds are you may not have the money to do so.

Fortunately, there are plenty of different ways you can go about getting someone else to pay for part of your real estate investment property.

Before you move forward with deciding to purchase a real estate property, consider the following tips for paying for your real estate investment:

Tip #1 Be an attractive borrower

While not everyone is going to have an excellent credit score to fall back on, there is still plenty you can do in order to maximize your borrowing position in the eyes of perspective lenders.

The best place to start is by considering the tools at your disposal which means you will want to start by checking your credit report and then seeking professional help if it isn't where you want it to be.

This is only the tip of the iceberg, however, as it is much more difficult to secure a loan for an investment property these days than it was in the days before the Great Recession.

This is especially true if you don't have a long credit history or lots of investment experience but, luckily, there are still plenty of options for those looking to secure the best deals when it comes to getting a loan for a real estate property.

Tip #2 Know your credit score: Generally speaking, you are going to need a credit score of 700 or better to get a private money lender to even talk to you.

In addition, having a credit score of 740 will ensure that you aren't paying higher than average interest fees.

Other than that, you can expect to see your interest rate go up about two points for every 10 points your credit score drops below this number.

The only other option if you have a score of lower than 740 is to accept a higher interest rate.

In addition, you will need to have money in your bank to pay for expenses for six months as part of the lending process.

So, if you have any investments and money saved up you can use this to help you secure a loan for purchasing a real estate property.

Tip #3 Stats and figures: Before you go ahead and reach out to any private money lenders, you are going to want to ensure you are prepared to show a complete list of all your expenses, as well as your current investment portfolio if applicable.

You will also need to be prepared to show proof of income for the past six months of an amount that can comfortably pay all of your bills as well as a financial stockpile good for three months' worth of bills including your loan payments of course.

These are standard requirements for most loans, though what you are required to provide for a complete loan is likely to be much more involved.

When it comes to finding a private money lender to work with, it can be tempting to take the first one that comes along that will agree to work with you.

However, doing so is a mistake as not being picky at this point in time can leave you will far fewer profits in the long-term.

As such, when a private money lender is interviewing you, use the time to also interview them as well.

Be sure to determine the total number of investors they are working with, the number of loans they allow for at one time, and the types of real estate they primarily provide loans for.

These questions will help you to get a feel for the private money lender and determine if you are on the same page when it comes to your future investment opportunities, not based on a sales pitch but based on the actual facts of the situation.

As an added bonus, having a complete understanding of what a private money lender is looking for will make it easier for you to change your approach of asking for a loan in order to improve your odds of securing a good deal on a loan.

#4 The right down payment: These days most traditional lending institutions will require that you put down 20 percent of the cost of the property you are hoping to purchase.

If you are looking to work with a hard money lender, then you may need to anticipate having twice that much on hand.

It is also interesting to keep in mind that being able to put down more than the minimum is key if you want to see the most favorable interest rates possible.

Having a down payment that is higher than the minimum is also an excellent way to ensure that the lender is able to overlook things like a less than ideal credit score.

If you don't think you can come up with 20 percent of the property you are interested in, but you qualify for a bank loan in every other way, then you may want to consider getting two mortgages in the realm of what you can afford and getting started that way.

While this will certainly get your foot in the door, it is vital that you pay off one of the mortgages as quickly as possible if you hope to see any type of profit any time soon.

*Tip #5 **Think locally:*** If you aren't the most attractive buyer at the moment then you may find that you have better success with smaller lenders than with the more traditional financial institutions.

Local private money lenders are a great choice for those individuals who have less than perfect credit scores or who have less than 20 percent to put down as the money lenders in these establishments are going to be far more likely to factor in the benefits of keeping the money in the local community and reduce the qualifications for the borrower which means you will more likely be able to secure a loan.

Another option that is surprisingly viable these days is **owner financing** which tends to be more effective these days than ever before.

Prior to the real estate troubles of the past decade, asking for **owner financing** was liable to make a seller think twice about dealing with you in the first place because of how eager banks were to give out home loans, especially to new buyers.

However, this has all changed to the point that recent estimates say that more than 20 percent of all sellers are open to the idea of **owner financing**.

If you can lock down **owner financing** then you will sign a promissory agreement that outlines how long it is going to take you to pay the seller back and the interest rate you will pay for the length of the repayment process.

Finding the Right Money Lender

If you are hoping that your first rental property is just going to be one of many then you will want to take the extra time early on to find a money lender that you can build a long-term relationship with.

This will, in turn, make it far easier for both of you to come up with a joint strategy that helps everyone come out on top, not just once but every time you find a new property to buy.

You will want to be cautious about dealing with real estate brokers, however, as they tend to be far more strict when it comes to the types of properties you are allowed to purchase.

Don't forget, the money lender is the person who is responsible for distributing your loans which means you are going to want to interview them directly before you sign anything.

Worthwhile questions to ask include thinks like the total number of investors the lender is working with, the number of separate loans you could have active at a single time and the type of real estate investments they work with most frequently.

Questions like these will make it easier for you to choose the right money lender with confidence because you will be looking at facts and not sales pitches.

Remember, there is nothing wrong with not choosing a money lender that you don't like as long as you don't drag the process out longer than you should and waste everyone's time as a result.

If you simply can't seem to find a money lender that fits your needs it is important to not settle for less than the best and simply to keep looking for a money lender that fits your needs.

Hard Money Loans

If you don't qualify for or are simply not interested in a traditional bank loan then your best place to look when it comes to rental property financing is a **hard money loan**.

This type of loan is simply one that is funded by at least one private investor rather than a more traditional financial institution.

These types of loans are often given for much shorter periods of time overall and a majority of your upfront payments will be used to pay off interest until a final major payment clears up the remainder principal on the loan.

Here are some tips for obtaining a **Hard Money Loan**:

Tip #1 Easier to acquire: Hard money loans tend to be especially attractive to new real estate investors as the lender is far more likely to assess the deal they are trying to make as opposed to their personal qualifications.

When it comes to finding a quality hard money lender, the first place you are going to want to go is to the local real estate investment club.

When it comes to finding out the real details on the local real estate scene there is no better place to start than with a local real estate club.

If you haven't yet, finding a local real estate club in most cities is as easy as doing a quick search online.

Even if you aren't looking for financing at the moment it is still a good idea to seek out a local real estate club to make it easier for you to learn the ropes regarding real estate investing as there are countless things a good real estate club can teach you.

Tip #2 Finding the right hard money lender:
When it comes to finding your perfect hard money lender, the first thing you will want to keep in mind is the fact that they tend to specialize in specific types of real estate deals which means you will want to determine if you are making a good decision of pursuing a hard money lender or if you are simply wasting your time.

Additionally, it is important to understand that these types of deals are almost always going to be of the first lien position variety.

What this means is that if things don't go exactly as you might have planned the first lien holder can expect to get all of their investment back before you get anything.

Generally speaking, determining the type of interest rate you can get along with a hard money loan is largely going to vary based on what state you are located in, how many other hard money lenders are operating in your area and the state of the market as a whole.

Regardless, the rates are always going to be steeper than if you were going through a traditional financial institution and will typically land somewhere in the range of 10 to 15 percent with the specifics dictating where precisely on the spectrum you fall.

From there, you can expect points to range somewhere between two and four percent of the total cost of the loan.

Tip #3 Value to loan ratio: The value to loan ratio is the total amount that a hard money lender will lend you for a given property.

The value to loan ratio can be determined by starting with the amount of the loan you are requesting and then dividing that number by the total estimated value of the property once it has been renovated and is in good condition.

Most hard money lenders won't agree to a loan that is more than 65 or 76 percent of the total value of the property once everything is said and done.

Alternately, some hard money lenders might instead base their amount on the worth of the property before renovations have been completed.

In some instances, you will be able to find a hard money lender that is interested in paying for most, if not all, of the property and may even pay for some of the renovation costs as well.

These types of loans are about as risky as you might expect which means they are going to expect as much as a 20 percent return on their investment in addition to other long-term commitments.

However, while the cost of the loan is certainly high, if there is no other way for you to move forward and obtain a loan then this can still be a great way to invest in your first real estate property with no money down.

Tip #4 Requirements for value to loan ratio: Generally speaking, the first thing you are going to need to do when you approach a hard money lender is to try to get a real estate deal that offers high returns and has the potential for a low risk investment.

Beyond that, however, you are going to want to do everything you can to ensure your finances are in order.

You will need a credit score that is no lower than 600, a debt/income ratio that is less than 45 percent and a credit history devoid of bankruptcies and foreclosures.

You will also need to be ready to prove that you can afford the added costs associated with the real estate property if it is not rented out.

In addition, you will also have to show that you are putting in a significant amount of equity into the real estate property to justify your stake in the property in the first place.

You will also need equity to back up the loan that the money lender will provide to you in case you fail to meet your financial obligations.

This can be handled via things like recent bank statements, tax returns, property appraisals, contracts of sales and repair estimates.

You will also need to do your best to provide a business plan that is air tight to show that you know best when it comes to the property in question.

If you present your information to the money lender in a clear and concise manner you can expect an answer regarding your request for a loan in as little as three weeks.

Other Options for Obtaining a Loan
Here are some tips for other options regarding obtaining a loan for a real estate property:

Tip #1 Ask the Federal Housing Administration for a loan: While it may seem surprising, in certain circumstances you can request that the federal government help finance your real estate investment.

The Federal Housing Administration (FHA) guidelines forbid loans for purely investment properties but if you intend to live in one unit of a multi-unit property then obtaining a loan from the Federal Housing Administration is definitely possible.

To qualify for a Federal Housing Administration loan, you only need to have 3.5 percent of the total cost of the real estate property for a down payment though you must then pay a separate private mortgage insurance each month.

For more information on Federal Housing Administration loans visit the website for the U.S. Department of Housing and Urban Development (HUD.com).

Tip #2 Save as much money as you can: If you think you may be close to having enough money to secure a down payment on your own for a real estate property then make sure you take the time to consider all options before deciding to do so.

If you already own a home then the equity it has accrued might be enough to use as a down payment for a real estate property.

In addition, using credit cards or certain forms of life insurance policies can also help you secure a down payment on a real estate property.

If you intend to look further into these types of options, ensure that your real estate investment is extremely profitable and worthwhile as your real estate investment can easily lead to undue financial hardship if not considered carefully.

Tip #3 Look into peer-to-peer lending sites: With the ever-growing popularity of crowd-funding as a successful means of starting a business, it would be foolish to assume lending money is still solely in the hands of big banks.

Peer lending sites including LendingClub.com and Prosper.com allow private citizens to lend and more importantly borrow money for almost anything they desire.

You simply put your details into the system which then assigns you a score which determines the rates of the loan you are asking for.

If you have already done your homework and are confident that your investment will see positive returns, share it with a peer lending site and see if anyone agrees to give you a loan.

Chapter 4: Landlord Considerations

Deciding What to Charge

When you are ready to decide what you are going to charge for your rental, the first thing you will want to consider is what is the current average rental price for similar properties in your area.

From there you will want to take what you paid for the property into account, especially if you are going to be making payments on the property as you will ideally be able to have the renter cover the price of the mortgage while still making a monthly profit after paying the property management company as well.

With that in mind, it is important to also understand that every single rental is different which means that if you feel there is something special about your property that really sets it apart, then you should ensure that the price reflects that as well.

Additionally, it is important to keep in mind that you never want to sell yourself short, as if you do, you are going to be stuck with an undervalued rental until the current tenant moves out.

Generally speaking, you will want to shoot for a rent that is roughly one percent of the total that you paid for the property.

Ideally this means a $100,000 property would rent for $1,000, and a $200,000 property would rent for $2,000 etc.,

Outside of any unique qualities, when it comes to classifying your real estate property you are going to want to break it into one of four different levels depending on the broad classification you can use to describe it and the various levels of classifications that are described below.

1) *A level properties:* The first type of properties, A level properties, are those that will attract a premium level of tenants who are going to be willing to pay top dollars and stay in one place for what could very easily be a prolonged period of time.

These properties are going to be in very nice neighborhoods with low crime or near extremely popular amenities which means they are always going to sit empty for a very short period of time.

You can typically get away with charging a smaller percentage of the total price than you would for other types of properties, simply because properties are never going to struggle to find renters.

2) **B level properties:** B level or Second tier properties will make up a majority of the properties you will see.

B level properties will be in average neighborhoods and will be good investments but will lack the eye-catching style and flair of tier one properties.

You will typically want to charge the standard one-percent per month rental fees for these properties as they are likely to end up sitting empty from time to time, though never for too long.

3) *C level properties:* C level or third tier properties are going to be those properties that need more work up front, and even then, they still aren't going to be anything special.

C level properties are typically in less desirable or unsafe areas and will often sit empty for long periods of time between occupants.

While these properties are typically going to be priced at less than $100,000, you are going to want to charge more for rent, not less.

A good rule of thumb for these properties is a two percent monthly rental fee which means rent on an $80,000 home would be $1,600, a $70,000 home would rent for $1,400 etc.,

To make up for the higher rental price you can compromise by being more relaxed and flexible when it comes to the leasing terms and who you will accept as a tenant.

4) *D level properties:* D level or fourth level properties are going to be properties that are at the bottom of the barrel when it comes to real estate properties.

These properties will be in poor and dangerous communities and many times these properties can remain vacant for long periods of time simply because no one wants to live in this housing and community.

It is important to state that these types of fourth level properties you really want to stay away from because you can actually end up losing a lot of money.

In addition, it is simply not worth it to invest in this type of real estate property because you may have high costs with maintaining the property as a result of the property being vandalized and because the rent may be too low to even make a profit.

Choosing the Right Tenants

Once you have been able to secure your first real estate property, now all you need to do is choose the right tenants that won't turn your dream of financial investment into a nightmare.

You are actually very close to begin the process of getting a return on your real estate investment. What is important now is that you choose your tenants wisely.

Simply, be firm in your tenant screening process and you will be reaping the rewards of profiting from your real estate investment sooner than you might think.

The main profit problems many landlords run into is not thoroughly screening their tenants. Therefore, you must make tenant screening a priority when deciding to rent out your real estate property.

Your investment can only be profitable when your tenants pay their rent on time and do not damage your property.

Even if you require a security deposit to cover any damages, the overhead and time it takes to manage the repairs at your property will eat away at your income.

It is important to state that there are options to check out future tenant's bill-paying habits by simply running a credit report.

You can also verify a future tenant's income as well as review their bank statements. In addition, you can also see if a future tenant has a criminal history by running a criminal background check and contacting their former landlords.

Now, there are many real estate investors and landlords that do not follow these basic practices when it comes to screening a tenant.

You can actually do quality background and credit checks for as low as $15. This investment is worth it to avoid losses from possible dangerous activity or non-paying tenants.

Remember, a responsible tenant will have a verifiable bill-paying history and have a noncriminal background.

Conducting a thorough tenant screening process will give you the best scenario for building a great landlord-tenant relationship and maximizes your cash flow.

The screening policy that works for each landlord is different based on personal preferences and the level of risk each landlord is comfortable with.

What matters the most, however, is that you have standards in place when screening a future tenant and that you stick to them each time you are presented with the opportunity to find a new tenant.

Without a firm set of standards, you run the risk of accepting anyone who can sign a lease, which can be a potentially disastrous position to be in, especially if you are working with your first rental property.

Here are some additional tips for screening a future tenant:

- Make sure the future tenant has No previous evictions. This should be both obvious and non-negotiable.

- Obtain work references from employers and previous landlords whenever possible.

- Make sure that the future tenant has a background check that comes back clean. The exact specifics are up to you, but no felonies or even misdemeanors are recommended when it comes to choosing your first tenant.

74

- Make sure the future tenant has reliable income. A rule of thumb is the future tenant should have an income of 3 times the rent of the rental property.

While you can be more specific if you like, you will often find that these tips for screening a future tenant will drastically improve the overall quality of the tenants that you see.

In addition, when it comes to actively screening people who come to look at the property, consider following these steps below:

The Lease

Once you have found a tenant that meets your qualifications, the next step is to create a lease that you can both live with which also clearly protects your rights as a landlord while also taking the tenants' rights into consideration as well.

In order to create a lease where both you the landlord and the tenant will agree to, it is important to make sure to write down all important details that are important to you regarding renting out your property.

At the same time, don't over do it but make sure that the lease lets the future tenant know what you expect from him/her when renting out your property.

When in doubt, put all important information in the lease in order to avoid any future problems when renting out your property.

By making sure everything is nice and clear upfront when renting out your property to a future tenant, you will feel more comfortable renting out your property because you are making the future tenant aware of your expectations when it comes to renting out your property.

At the same time the future tenant will have a clear understanding of your expectations and will more likely respect the lease and the rental property as a result of you being open and direct about your expectations.

Keep this in mind, **studies show that tenants are more than twice as likely to follow rules that are clearly laid out in front of them ahead of time in writing as opposed to those rules that are only ever mentioned in passing.**

Also keep in mind that your real estate property represents a major investment and this process of having a detailed lease will help make it easier for you to keep it in an ideal state for as long as humanly possible.

In addition to the things that are and are not allowed in the lease, it is important to have a very clear list of consequences for what will occur when things that are not allowed take place.

The following tips are a good place to start if you aren't sure what to include on the lease:

Tip #1 The deposit: Always request a deposit from a tenant. You can legally request the first and last month's rent as a deposit from a tenant before they move into the property.

The deposit amount will depend on how much the rent is and the area your property is located in.

The "last" month's rent can also be seen as a deposit too but be clear about the deposit with the tenant especially when the tenant moves out.

Something to keep in mind is that the money taken as a deposit is to be used for repairs based on damage done by the renter.

This is usually referred to as something that is not "reasonable." Yes, carpets get dirty and paint from a wall may be slightly marked up due to a person moving furniture in or out of the rental property.

However, damage done because a renter smashed their fist through a wall because they were upset, or the renter's dog damaged the carpet by chewing on it or someone spray painted on the walls are all unreasonable damages of a rental property.

As a result, a deposit is meant to cover property damages and other issues that are not reasonable or may even be considered deliberate damages by the renter.

Obtaining a deposit from a tenant is also good idea because you want to make sure that the renter does not neglect paying you the monthly rent.

Believe it or not, but there have actually been people, tenants, who sneak out at night because they cannot pay the rent, yet these people still demand the return of their first and last month's rent deposit that they made.

So, by securing at least two month's deposit to protect yourself if there is a late rental payment, a missed payment, or someone moves out without prior notice is a sort of "insurance" and protection of your real estate property and investment.

Tip #2 Pets: You have to decide if you are you going to allow pets or not into your rental property.

Actually, many of the large apartment complexes owned by large real estate investment groups do not allow pets for personal reasons.

These large real estate investment groups are unwilling to lose the profit it takes to clean an apartment after a pet has been inside a rental property.

In addition, sometimes there is also a higher chance for multiple units to be empty at the same time when a pet is allowed inside a rental property.

If apartment complexes decide to allow pets, then fees are going to be astronomical for both renting and managing the property.

A renter may be required to pay as much as $400 for a pet deposit, per pet. In addition, the renter may also be charged an additional fee called "pet rent" per month, which can be anywhere from $10 to $100 a month, per pet.

A person really has to love their pets to want to pay a high price for renting out a property that charges such high fees.

Sometimes, there is also an issue of how many pets a tenant can have while renting out a property.

Typically, the maximum number of pets a tenant may have is two. There may also be some restrictions on the breed of the dog as well as some size restrictions in many apartment complexes.

Something to keep in mind is that when a person moves out, if the unit needs a deeper cleaning because their pet left an odor or there was damage to doors or walls, then there may be an issue with the renter losing their entire deposit.

This is why some apartment complexes have weighed the risk of having pets against the costs they incur and decline to allow pets.

For a person trying to rent a single property, there may be other considerations to be made. **Here are some other considerations listed below:**

1. If a pet damages the carpet, you either need to have it cleaned or remove it and replace it with new carpeting.

2. If damage occurs to the doors, windows, floor tile or anywhere else in the property due to the pet, you have to fix it.

3. You are usually renting a property in a neighborhood, which the community may not be happy if a loud animal continually makes noise throughout the day and night.

4. You may lose more than 50% of the possible renters or tenants who are looking to rent a property.

As you can, there are some risks when it comes to allowing pets into your rental property.

*Tip #3 **Late rent:*** It is also very important to consider how you are going to go about ensuring that tenants make a point of paying their rent on time.

While you don't need to be excessively harsh on your tenants when they don't pay the rent on time you are well within your rights to charge a "late fee" to ensure that paying the rent late isn't something that is going to happen too frequently.

Making sure a tenant pays the rent on time is one of the most important parts of any lease.

In addition, if you include a "late fee" clause on the lease then a tenant may end up paying you hundreds and maybe even thousands more as a result of constantly paying the rent late.

Generally speaking, the best way to eliminate a tenant from paying the rent late is by instituting a fee that is either based on a set amount or a portion of the rent.

You may also want to take a look at any local laws on the topic of tenants that pay the rent late.

However, most of the time you should be largely free to set your own rules in this regard which means you could even charge a fee that increases based on how late the rent ultimately ends up being paid.

You will want to ensure the amount is high enough that it is meaningful to the renter while not being so harsh that it makes it likely the next month's rent is going to be late as well.

Tip #4 When and why you can enter the property: While not something you are likely going to have to do very often, it is of vital importance that if you have a real need to enter the property that a tenant is renting from you, then you are freely allowed to do so.

This is, of course, a very thin line to walk because if you give the tenants too much power then you run the risk of being in a situation where you would be unable to protect your real estate investment if the worst were to occur.

However, on the other hand you need to ensure that prospective tenants feel as though they would be comfortable in their new home without having the landlord disturb them for no reason.

The best middle of the road action is to offer a 48-hour notice to your tenants before being able to enter the property on official business.

Tip #5 Don't forget the garbage: While this one falls under the label of things that most people wouldn't expect to have to spell out, the fact of the matter is that some tenants will need strict rules when it comes to keeping your property trash free.

In addition to hurting the value of your real estate property, the issue of having trash piled up around your property could escalate into you receiving fines from the city which means it is important to clearly lay out your expectations from your tenant for have a garbage free property.

Tip #6 Make it clear that respecting the neighbors is required: While not required in the strictest sense, this clause will only make your life easier in the long-term as if you have rude or noisy tenants then you are the one who is sure to hear about it from the neighbors.

Simply if you value your sanity then you will want to do everything in your power in order to ensure the neighbors don't have any complaints when it comes to your choice of tenants.

As a result, make sure you include noise guidelines in the lease as well as any other caveats that you feel your neighbors will appreciate right from the start and you will never have any issues with your neighbors or your tenants.

Chapter 5: Turnkey Rental Property

A turnkey property is a property that is purchased under the guarantee, either written or implied, that the property will start generating a cash flow as soon as the contract is signed. Many turnkey properties even come with renters already included with the deal.

Unlike with a traditional property that you try and find for the best price possible, it is much more difficult to successfully negotiate for a turnkey property as everything is ready to go as far as putting it to work is concerned.

As a real estate investor, you have two different options when it comes to investing in turnkey rental properties depending on how quickly you want the process to be relatively hands off.

First of all, you have the option of finding a property that is in turnkey condition by yourself and then filling it with a qualified tenant who will hopefully stick around for as long as possible.

You will then want to find a property management company to manage the property for you on a daily basis for which they will take an estimated ten percent of each month's rent.

This way of operating a turnkey rental investment plan will also allow you to find properties for a cheaper price because they are not yet being marked up by a company who is trying to make as much money from each potential customer as possible.

On the downside, however, you will have to be more involved in the running of each turnkey property and you will have to deal with vacancies directly.

On the other hand, if you decide to seek out a turnkey rental property company to manage the property for you then you will have to a pay a premium for the property that you ultimately purchase as well as for the property management company that they work with to handle all of the issues that may come up with the property in question.

For this premium you can expect to purchase a turnkey property and then essentially sit back and let the profits roll in.

However, choosing a reliable turnkey rental property company can feel like a full-time job at certain moments because of all the research you will have to do to ensure you have left your real estate investment in reliable hands.

Actually, with this type of investment (turnkey property), you can typically expect to start seeing a return 30 days after you officially own the property.

Understanding the Risks of Owning a Turnkey Property

One of the biggest misconceptions that many individuals have about investing in real estate via turnkey properties is that every property that is labeled turnkey is automatically going to be a great real estate investment.

However, just because a turnkey property doesn't require renovation does not mean there is no reason to assume that it is automatically worth the asking price.

As such, you are going to want to apply just as much due diligence to any property that you are purchasing under the turnkey banner as you would any other investment that you make.

If you decide to look for a turnkey property on your own then this means you are going to want to get to know a local property inspector who you can call when it comes time to look for and inspect a turnkey property.

If you decide to use a turnkey company for helping you find a property then you are still going to want to go and physically see and inspect the property in question.

If for some reason you don't go and inspect the turnkey property you are considering to purchase then if the investment fails at a later date, you will only have yourself to blame.

Additionally, you are going to want to go above and beyond when it comes to researching the property management company or turnkey property company that you choose to work with.

More so than with many other types of real estate investments, the real estate company that you choose to work with is going to have a major impact on the overall success or failure of your turnkey real estate investment.

In addition, you need to be mindful of the real estate company that you choose to work when it comes to helping you find the right turnkey real estate investment for you.

This means you are going to want to have a clear idea of the overall level of experience the real estate company has, before deciding whether to hire them to help you with your pursuit of purchasing a real estate property.

Choose Your Real Estate Company Carefully

While real estate companies are often an important part of any real estate investment, nowhere is this going to be more important than with turnkey real estate companies.

Simply turnkey real estate companies are going to have a serious effect on the overall profitability of a turnkey property.

Something to keep in mind is that when working with a turnkey real estate company it is important to keep in mind that there are two primary types of transactions they are going to try and sell you on.

First, you will often find that you will have the option of purchasing the turnkey property outright, in much the same way as you would with any other type of real estate transaction. Now, this is the option you should always choose.

However, many turnkey real estate companies will also offer an alternative where they become your partner in an LLC.

An LLC is not a corporation but instead it is a legal form of a company that provides limited liability to its owners (you being the owner).

While this LLC alternative will require you to ultimately do even less work when owning and operating a turnkey property, in the long run, it puts your ownership of the property into an odd state of limbo and also makes it more difficult for you to sell the property at a later date.

In addition, this LLC alternative will also leave a potential opening for the turnkey company to pull something shady and as a result this option of having a LLC with a turnkey company should never be agreed to under normal circumstances.

While investing in a thoroughly vetted turnkey company is one of the most reliable types of real estate investments imaginable, that doesn't mean it doesn't come with the same inherent risks that any other type of real estate investment does.

As with any investment, if you want to know if investing in turnkey real estate is right for you, all you need to do is consider the potential profit and then determine if that justifies the related risk in your eyes and then act accordingly.

In order to choose the best turnkey rental property for you, the first thing you will have to do is limit your number of possible choices when it comes to choosing a turnkey real estate company as there are more than one thousand of these types of companies in the United States.

In addition, many of these turnkey real estate companies are designed to charge unaware investors a lot of money for their services so choose a company wisely.

As such, the first thing you are going to want to do when it comes to narrowing down your choices when choosing a turnkey real estate company is to eliminate the ones that don't have a physical address prominently featured on their website.

It is also important that you take the extra step and verify that the address of the turnkey real estate company is not simply a mailbox address.

The reason for this is simple, if things go wrong with your turnkey real estate investment then you need to know that you have a place you can go and hold someone accountable for the situation you may find yourself in.

In addition, by a turnkey real estate investment having a physical address, this will also prove that they aren't some fly-by-night operation and that they are actually a real company you may want to go into business with in the long-term.

It is important to state that there are many online-only turnkey real estate companies so the next step is to consider recommendations from your local real estate investment club or local real estate investment organization.

Consider this, you can also seek out online recommendations for turnkey real estate companies as long as you have some reason to assume the source is legitimate.

It is important to state that personal recommendations for turnkey real estate companies are important.

However, this doesn't mean you shouldn't do your own research when it comes to hiring a turnkey real estate company.

If you are looking for a turnkey real estate company in another city or state then you will definitely want to reach out to a local real estate club or organization for advice on where to start.

While a local real estate club or organization from other cities or states are unlikely to be as helpful as if you were not an outsider, they should at the very least be able to still point you in the right direction when it comes to hiring a turnkey real estate company.

Barring these types of recommendations, your best bet is to seek out turnkey companies that are both owned and operated locally as this means there are fewer levels of management that you need to worry about when working with these companies.

After you have found a few turnkey companies that may be potential candidates for working with you, the next step is going to be digging deeper into their business practices starting with client reviews.

When reading a turnkey company's online reviews, you don't need to worry about individual reviews but you should instead pay special attention to any trends you might see forming as you sort through the specifics.

If multiple people mention a specific negative aspect of the turnkey company and its services, then it is a surefire bet that there is some type of issue there that could deserve a closer look.

A good rule of thumb is to definitely consider any negative reviews you may come across regarding a specific turnkey company.

Beyond these types of negative patterns, you will also want to do what you can in order to ensure the company you choose meets a few additional requirements as well.

For starters, it is important that you choose a company that has been in business for a minimum of 10 years as anything less than this it is hard to know if the management has figured out the ins and outs of the real estate business yet.

Remember, if you decide to work with a turnkey company that has been in business for less than 10 years then the type of properties that they may have available may be inferior to what you might expect.

So, remember you want to work with a turnkey company that has over a decade of experience so that they can provide you with the best kind of real estate investment possible.

Something to also keep in mind is that a turnkey rental property is all about getting steady, reliable returns which means it is not the type of investment you want to take a risk on.

So, what this means is that if you want to make money quickly then simply use a turnkey company for helping you obtain a property so that you can begin to make a quick return on your real estate investment.

However, do NOT form an LLC with a turnkey company because you may not have much control of your real estate investment.

Another thing you want to consider when looking to work with a turnkey property is that you also want to look into their practices when it comes to things like property management and renovation as it is important that you agree with all aspects of the real estate project before you move forward with working with a turnkey company.

As you can see, all of this important information is data that can be verified by a third party which means you will want to avoid taking the company at face value on anything they say.

Not only will verifying a turnkey company by a third party makes it easier for you to ensure that the company in question ends up being truly honest, but it will also make it easier for you to guarantee that the company you ultimately choose has employees that are knowledgeable as well.

Once you find a few turnkey companies that you are interested in working with, the next step will be to talk to representatives from each company directly in order to get a better idea about how it really is to work with them.

The first test should be finding out how difficult it is for you to find the turnkey company's contact information you are looking for.

For example, if you have an emergency you want to be able to get in touch with the turnkey company as quickly as possible.

However, if you can't find a phone number for contacting the turnkey company then this sends a very clear message that the turnkey rental company cannot be trusted.

Another thing to consider about a turnkey company is that if there is a contact phone number available then you want to make sure the company is able to return your phone call within 24 hours of contacting.

If a turnkey company cannot return your phone within one business day, then this is a company you do not want to do business with.

While this may seem harsh, the fact of the matter is that if a turnkey company can't be bothered to return a phone call that could easily end in a sale of a real estate property of $100,000 or more then you need to ask yourself how likely they are to return your calls after you have gone ahead and made the decision of working with them.

Simply, either a turnkey company doesn't have the resources to get back to you in a reasonable amount of time or they don't have the motivation to do so, and either way, this represents a company you don't want in charge of your real estate investment.

Now keep this in mind, when you do speak to someone from a turnkey company it is important to be aware of their overall level of professionalism as this will directly reflect on how they are likely to treat their ongoing clients.

Furthermore, you can assume that a turnkey company's level of professionalism at this stage will directly translate into their professionalism with other, more vital, aspects of the company as well.

Therefore, this means that a turnkey company is more likely to be worth your time than a company whose employees answer the phone in an unprofessional manner.

Additionally, it is important to speak with the person working for the turnkey company who would be handling your real estate investment property directly if you do decide to give this company your business.

You will also want to make sure you speak with the contact person from the turnkey property multiple times before you decide to work with the company.

So, you always want to make sure the contact person from the turnkey company is friendly, reliable and professional at all times.

When speaking to the management personnel from the turnkey company you are looking to work with, it is important to do extensive research on the area and community you plan to purchase real estate property in.

By doing research on the area and community you plan to invest in beforehand, you will ensure that the management personnel from the turnkey company have up to date information on the area and the real estate market as a whole.

When choosing a few turnkey companies that you are most interested in working with, it is important to rely on more than just the data you have collected.

Therefore, you should also be able to ask the turnkey rental property for references and you should be sure to do so, especially if you didn't get any recommendations from any third parties.

If the turnkey company you are considering is unwilling or unable to provide these types of references to you then you may want to look for a different turnkey company to work with.

Once you have found a suitable turnkey company that you want to work with, it is then extremely important that you consider the level of support you are going to get from the company once you have given them money for investing in a specific real estate property.

Even if you've been taken care of quite well up to this point, there is nothing guaranteeing that things will continue to positively move forward with the turnkey company.

Something else that you also want to keep in mind is that, it is important to ensure that the turnkey company you are teaming up with doesn't outsource their property management tasks to another company.

If this is the case then you will need to do your due diligence on the third-party company in order to ensure that you will be as happy will them as you will be with the initial turnkey company.

Chapter 6: Tips for Success

The truth of the matter is that as long as you do your research on a potential real estate property and neighborhood before you go ahead and decide to purchase a piece of property, you will definitely make a profit on your investment.

You also want to make sure that you can still pay off any related debts on your real estate investment while still making a profit from it.

Here are some additional tips for succeeding at investing in real estate:

Tip #1 Start making money when you buy: While many new investors think that this statement means simply getting a good price on a real estate property, the reality is much more all-inclusive than that.

While getting a good price for a piece of real estate is certainly part of it, it is more about finding other ways you can get immediately increase the value from your real estate investment.

For example, you may renovate your real estate property in order to flip it and sell it for a profit or you can simply rent it out for a higher rental fee.

Therefore, definitely focus on trying to get a good deal on a real estate property when investing in real estate.

However, also consider that even if you don't get a good deal on a certain real estate property, simply figure out a way to invest additional money in your property in order to make more money by on it by flipping it or by simply renting it for a higher rental fee.

Tip #2 Focus on consistent residency: When you are looking for real estate properties, one of your biggest criteria should always be properties that you can expect to quickly and steadily attract tenants or to keep existing tenants for as long as possible.

Keep this in mind, as a buying and holding real estate investor, every month that a property sits empty is a month that you not only lose out on a profit on your investment but you actually have to pay out of pocket for property related expenses as well.

Tip #3 Know how involved you want to be from the start: If you are interested in being the person that your tenants always contact when something goes wrong with the property, then there is virtually no limit to what type of residential real estate you can invest in.

If, however, you are hoping for something a little "more hands off," then what you are instead going to want to consider is using a property management company for all your day to day landlord issues and duties.

Tip #4 Don't plan while viewing a property: If you find yourself making a plan regarding what you would do with a potential real estate property then simply stop planning.

What you want to do is make sure to do some research on the local area and real estate market before making any plans to purchase real estate property.

If you don't do any research on the local area or real estate market when viewing a property for the first time then you will have left yourself at a huge disadvantage when it comes to determining the right price to offer for the property.

Simply put, if you don't know what you are going to do with a property, you can't buy it for a price that will ensure you make money in the process unless you are very lucky.

It is important to state that many new real estate investors fall into the business by purchasing a property for a price that they feel is simply too good to pass up.

However, the reality of the matter is, if you haven't even done research on the local market, then you have no way of knowing a good deal, even when it is staring you in the face.

Therefore, you always want to remember the fact that just because a property is a good deal, doesn't mean that it is a good deal for you at that very moment.

Tip #5 Don't expect too much too soon: While you can realistically rent out a property in certain states in a matter of days, this is certainly the exception, not the rule.

As such, having an unrealistic time frame of how long it is going to be before your new real estate investment starts to turn a profit is crucial to being prepared both mentally and financially.

What' s more, the process of renting out a property can easily take much longer than expected, simply due to unexpected external factors that cropped up after you were already in the process of trying to turn a profit on the property.

While there are also several factors that can align to work in your favor, the point is that making a return on real estate is never going to happen quickly.

Instead, the benefits come from the fact that you will always make a profit given a long enough timeline simply because investing and profiting in real estate is a long-term process.

Tip #6 Don't overestimate your abilities: In many scenarios having faith in yourself that exceeds your actually ability is considered a positive character trait.

However, when it comes to investing in real estate, it is important to have a more "realistic view of yourself and the immediate success you will have.

Simply, to save time and money when it comes to investing in real estate you want to make sure to do a lot of research and to slowly and patiently go about the process of purchasing your first real estate property.

Specifically, this applies most frequently to new real estate investors who overestimate their personal ability to undertake or complete renovations in a timely manner on a given property.

Tip #7 Don't underestimate relationships: When it comes to successfully investing and succeeding in real estate it is important to keep in mind that even the most self-sufficient real estate investor is going to need to foster a few key relationships if they hope to be successful in the long run.

First and foremost, you are going to want to find a real estate agent that you can work with who you trust to find you the best real estate deals possible.

Depending on the type of real estate investing you are doing, the right real estate agent can cut down on the amount of work you have to do personally when it comes to finding properties, and can also find you better deals than you might otherwise have access to on your own.

Furthermore, if you plan on using loans to finance the early part of your real estate investment career then you are also going to want to find a local financial loan lender with competitive rates who you can build a mutually beneficial relationship with.

If you find a local financial loan lender with competitive rates then this should ultimately lead to better rates, which means more money in your pocket per investment property.

Additionally, you are also going to want a real estate lawyer you can count on, a home inspector who can be available on short notice and an appraiser you have a good relationship with.

Tip #8 Negotiation tips: When it comes to getting the best real estate deal possible, consider the following negotiation tips to give your deal a little extra boost:

- **Tip #1 Remain silent.** This is good advice regardless of how you are submitting offers or counter offers.

Simply, your response to an offer sets the tone for the remainder of the negotiations and if you take the time to simply act self-assured at your price offer while appearing completely comfortable with the silence then the other party has no choice but to respond positively to your price offer.

To seal the deal, repeat your current offer after 30 seconds of silence has passed, don't elaborate just repeat the facts. The likely response to this tactic is an acceptance of your offer from the other party.

- **Tip #2 Body language.** Take advantage of your body language and the other party's body language when discussing making a deal over a piece of real estate property you are interested in investing in.

Simply appear confident and be sure of yourself when making an offer on a real estate deal and don't retreat or go back on your offer.

Also, remember to stay firm, be polite and always appear and act confident.

Remember to also observe the other party's body language to see how they react to your firm, confident offer.

If the other party gets the feeling that you will not change your offer then they will most likely give in to your offer.

However, do be aware that it is very common for the other party to always counter your offer and try to secure a better deal for himself.

Nevertheless, do a lot of research on the property that you are looking to purchase as well as the company that you are negotiating with and go in with great confidence and you will be more than likely to secure a good deal for yourself.

- **Tip #3 Address Important Issues.** While everyone likes to win when coming out of a negotiation, when it comes to buying and investing in real estate, it is important to focus on any serious issues that may need addressing instead of squabbling over amounts under $10,000.

For example, the difference between a real estate property that is $200,000 and $205,000 is only $21 per month.

Therefore, take the demands the other party asks of you seriously and determine their true costs before committing to purchasing and investing in real estate.

It is also important to remember that the real estate property is what is truly at stake regarding your negotiations and not to let the perfect real estate property slip away from you as a result of not coming to some sort of agreement.

- **Tip #4 Ask for concessions.** Regardless of whether or not the area you are looking to invest in real estate can be considered a "buyer's market," it is important to ask the seller of the property for concessions, including repairs, and renovations that may be needed.

Tip# 5 Always read contracts thoroughly: A lifetime of simply clicking agree on hundreds and hundreds of electronic user agreements has made most people far too trusting when it comes to accepting and agreeing to contracts.

Unfortunately, the level of personal importance you will derive from a contract for your first rental property and that of your new smartphone are vastly different which is why it is so important to treat real estate contracts like the important documents that they are.

This is why it is so important to take the time you need to understand the finer points of any contracts you sign, either regarding a loan for a real estate property or the property itself.

Failing to take the time to fully understand the contract of a loan for a real estate property or the property itself is similar to gambling with your long-term real estate investment.

Simply, by not taking the time to read a contract thoroughly can easily cause you to end up paying significantly more than you expected and you will have no one to blame for the extra cost but yourself.

Conclusion

Thanks for making it through to the end of this rental property investing book.

Hopefully, this book was informative and able to provide you with all of the information you need regarding purchasing and investing in real estate.

Something to keep in mind is that you always have to keep learning about the ever-changing real estate market.

In addition, always do research on a piece of real estate that you are interested in investing in as well as any company that you decide to do business with when in comes to investing in real estate.

While investing in real estate can most definitely help you to generate a lifetime of passive income, it is important to have the right expectations when you first get started if you want to succeed with real estate investing.

First, it is important to understand that it takes a lot of time and effort to create a passive income stream when it comes to investing in real estate.

In addition, it can be said that you will always have to be aware of your real estate investment and the maintenance of your property which means there is nothing passive about investing in real estate.

Likewise, doing the required research to find the right neighborhood and the right property within that neighborhood isn't something that is going to happen overnight, it is going to take serious dedication and planning before you start seeing traction in your chosen real estate investment.

In addition, you can always hire a management company to manage your real estate property but it also takes time and effort to hire a good management company and maintain a good working relationship with that company.

However, you will eventually get to a place where the amount of time and energy you have to put in on your real estate investment will be far less and you will begin to reap the profits of your real estate investment.

Thus, it is important to not lose faith when the going gets tough and to instead remember that successful real estate investment is like a marathon as opposed to a sprint which means that slow and steady wins the race.

Thanks again for taking the time to read through my book and I wish you great success with your real estate investing endeavors.

www.ingramcontent.com/pod-product-compliance
Lightning Source LLC
Chambersburg PA
CBHW072147170526
45158CB00004BA/1538